EVERGLADES

BY
Christine Sotnak Rom

I wish to thank the Interpretive Staff of Everglades National Park for all their help.

PUBLISHED BY
CRESTWOOD HOUSE
Mankato, MN, U.S.A.

CIP

LIBRARY OF CONGRESS CATALOGING IN PUBLICATION DATA

Rom, Christine Sotnak.
  Everglades

  (National parks)
  Includes index.
  SUMMARY: Describes the plant and animal life found in the swampy area of the Florida Everglades and discusses the park located there.
  1. Zoology — Florida — Everglades National Park — Juvenile literature. 2. Botany — Florida — Everglades National Park — Juvenile literature. 3. Natural history — Florida — Everglades National Park — Juvenile literature. 4. Everglades National Park (Fla.) — Juvenile literature.[1. Zoology — Florida — Everglades National Park. 2. Botany — Florida — Everglades National Park. 3. Everglades National Park (Fla.) 4. National parks and reserves.] I. Title. II. Series: National parks (Mankato, Minn.)
  QH105.F6R65   1988   508.759'39 — dc19   88-18644
  ISBN 0-89686-404-9

International Standard Book Number:	Library of Congress Catalog Card Number:
0-89686-404-9	88-18644

PHOTO CREDITS

Cover: Bill Allen
DRK Photo: (Stephen J. Krasemann) 11, 16-17, 24, 42-43; (C. C. Lockwood) 12-13; (Doug Perrine) 34
Bill Allen: 4, 6, 8-9, 19, 27, 28, 32-33, 40-41
Tom Stack: (Rod Planck) 20; (Brian Parker) 22, 39; (Matt Bradley) 29
Journalism Services: (Richard Day) 7, 15, 31, 37; (Max & Bea Hunn) 10

Produced by Carnival Enterprises.

CRESTWOOD HOUSE

Box 3427, Mankato, MN, U.S.A. 56002

TABLE OF CONTENTS

Everglades National Park

ENTERING THE EVERGLADES

Hundreds of years ago, the Everglades was an area of great mystery, beauty, and danger. Early Spanish explorers feared the swamp. The endless waterways and muddy sinkholes looked sinister and mysterious to the explorers. They had known people to enter the swamp and never be seen or heard from again.

It seemed to the explorers that the blades of razor-sharp sawgrass went on forever. Poisonous snakes slithered silently, looking for prey. Giant alligators, 15 feet long, lurked below the still waters. The air was thick with swarms of hungry mosquitoes.

Today, part of the Everglades is a national park where thousands of people come each year. Now visitors can take trips with reasonable safety into Everglades National Park and see its wonders.

Much of the beauty and some of the dangers still remain. Time and civilization have done much to change the Everglades from hundreds of years ago. Adventures still await visitors to this tropical wilderness.

Many parts of the Everglades are covered in a tangle of grass, plants, and trees.

The Everglades' swamp water flows slowly across plains of sawgrass to the Gulf of Mexico.

ACRES OF SWAMP LAND

The swampland of Florida's Everglades is unique to southern Florida. It is a low, flat plain that mixes with the sea. The water, which is so necessary to the swampland's wildlife, is supplied by heavy rainfall. Florida's warm weather provides the perfect climate for the rare plants and animals that live in this area.

The name "Everglades" comes from the Old English saxon word "glyde," which means bright, shimmering place in a forest. The Everglades is in fact a wide, flat river. The river begins at Lake Okeechobee (pronounced O-kee-cho-bee), a large lake in the center of Florida, and ends in the Gulf of Mexico and the Florida Bay. The river is about 120 miles long, 40 miles wide, and

FUN FACT The tender base of a sawgrass can be okay to eat. Just peel back the outer skin and take a bite after a park ranger shows you how.

only 2 feet deep. The water flows slowly across the plains of sawgrass, sloughs, hammocks, and tropical forests.

The Seminole Native Americans, who still live in parts of the Everglades, call the watery plains of sawgrass Pa-ha-okee, which means "grassy water." These sawgrass plains are laced with hundreds of human-made *canals*. The canals are surrounded by plants and little islands of trees. Many Native Americans call these *island hammocks,* which some say means "trees that float." Others say that hammock is a Spanish word meaning "garden place."

In the Everglades, the scenery is always changing. The more you explore the wonders within the park, the more you will discover. It is truly a land of changing life and ever-flowing glydes.

Canoeists can enjoy the shade of "island hammocks."

Cypress trees draped in hanging Spanish moss grow along the water's edge.

TREES OF THE EVERGLADES

The trees found in the Everglades tell a tale of their own. In the past, one of the wonders in the swamp was the mighty cypress tree. It had withstood fires and hurricane winds for centuries. The oldest group of bald cypress

trees was draped in hanging Spanish moss.

Some of these trees were 600 to 700 years old! Two hundred years before Columbus landed in North America, some bald cypress trees were already 100 feet high. Today most of those mighty trees are gone. The ones that are left are called pond cypress. Others are called dwarf cypress trees. When fully grown, these trees are only three to four feet tall!

FUN FACT   The poisonwood tree found in the Everglades is related to the poison ivy plant. It is very irritating to the skin and causes a red, itching rash.

Some birds use the "knees" of the cypress tree to hold their nests.

Cypress trees have pointed roots that stick up through the water. These are called *cypress knees*. They often make good perches for nesting birds.

Many living things make themselves at home on the cypress trees. In just one tree you might see long, slithering snakes, hanging vines, huge spider webs, wild orchids, trumpet creepers, and sweet-smelling Jasmine flowers.

Other strange and lovely trees are seen in the Everglades. A forest of custard apple trees grows on the south and east shores of Lake Okeechobee. The custard apple is a favorite food of turtles. Nearby, clear ponds are surrounded by arched ceilings of ash maple trees. The trees grow so thick that only a small amount of sunlight finds its way into the jungle.

Down by the seashore where the water turns salty, mangrove forests flourish. Salt water doesn't hurt mangrove trees. In fact, they actually ooze salt from their leaves. To help its roots breathe better in salty water, a black

FUN FACT Between 1940 and 1950, an estimated 36,000 trainloads of cypress logs were cut from the cypress swamp and hauled away for lumber.

mangrove tree sends up little straw-like roots to help it get more air. Sometimes during a windy day at low tide, the mangrove drops its seeds into the mud. The heavy ends stick upright and begin to grow into mangrove seedlings.

Mangrove trees are land builders. Their arched, claw-like roots are called *prop roots*. They catch and hold soil. That helps the tree stand up to hurricane winds. In the salty water, shell-encased tree oysters cling to the prop roots of the red mangrove. This tree also provides homes for wild animals. Under an umbrella of mangrove branches, wild bobcats and raccoons live and hunt.

Farther into the hammocks, the royal palm grows tall and straight. Beneath its heavy crown of dark green leaves hang little clusters of fruits. They look a little like jewels in a crown.

One of the Everglades' most interesting trees is the gumbo limbo tree. This tree has bright, copper-colored bark that peels away from the tree like

Mangrove trees use their prop roots to secure themselves in the soil.

Throughout the Everglades, mangrove trees grow in saltwater.

sunburned skin. Native Americans used the sticky *resin* from the tree to make ointments and incense. When these trees were young, the wood was so soft that people used it to carve horses for merry-go-rounds or wooden floats for fishing nets.

The gumbo limbo tree seems to have many lives. If it blows over in a hurricane, any part that still touches the ground sends out roots and keeps on growing.

BEAUTIFUL BIRDS

The Everglades is home to thousands of birds. The trees are dotted with color as palm warblers, snowy egrets, and roseate spoonbills enjoy the treasures of the swamp.

Once, early in this century, hunters nearly wiped out the snowy egrets and the roseate spoonbills. The snowy egret's long, white feathers and the great egret's plumes were in great demand for ladies' hats. People worried that soon these lovely birds would disappear forever. As a result, in 1947, President Truman declared that the Everglades National Park would be a bird sanctuary. Now thousands of birds are protected by law, free to live and nest without fear of human hunters.

One strange bird called the limpkin, has a wild, wailing cry. This dark brown, speckled bird uses its long legs for wading in the pond. Here it picks out a feast of snails with its long bill.

Birds of the Everglades spend most of their time hunting for food. The great blue heron spears fish with its long, pointed bill. The red-shouldered hawk perches in a tree and waits to swoop down on prey.

The bird with the most peculiar fishing style is the anhinga, or snake bird. The snake bird is named for its long, snake-like neck. When it swims underwater only its head shows. It spears a fish with its beak, then tosses it into the air so it can catch and swallow it head first.

In the early morning, the Everglades wakes to the sights and sounds of nesting birds. Hawks, eagles, and vultures search for prey. Bright, purple gallinules preen their feathers with quick, orange beaks. The black man-o-war shows off its great, hooked bill and stretches its eight-foot wings in flight. In mid-flight, the black skimmer snatches fish out of the water with

FUN FACT The green-backed heron likes to go fishing for a meal. It wades into the water and drops a leaf or twig into the water. When a fish comes close to see what fell in the water, the green-backed heron snaps it up.

The white ibis is one of the many amazing birds found in the Everglades.

Flocks of roseate spoonbills live in the Everglades' quiet coves.

16

its lower beak.

Brown pelicans nest on the mangrove islands, stretching their wings as much as nine feet across. Pelicans are one of southern Florida's largest birds. A pelican holds its fish in a deep pouch in its beak.

Bright pink flamingos are occasionally seen visiting southern Florida. They never stay to nest in the Everglades. After a short rest they fly further south to Cuba, Haiti, or the Bahamas, making bright bands of color across the sky.

The snail kite is a clever bird somewhat like a hawk. With bright, keen eyes it can catch food and drink water while flying. Sadly, it is in danger of vanishing from the Everglades. That's because its only food, the apple snail, is becoming harder to find.

Another bird that someday may vanish from the Everglades is the wood stork. This long-legged bird is America's only native stork. It is very busy during nesting time; it never returns to the nest without a fish for its young or a stick to add to its nest.

In the evening twilight, when the day is almost over, visitors to the Everglades can look up and see hundreds of birds. The air is filled with the soft whirr of wings. Bird voices blend in concert, adding music to the Everglades.

SWEET-SMELLING FLOWERS

In spring and summer, the Everglade hammocks often look like a fairytale land. Blossoming clusters of sweet-smelling flowers spring to life after a rain shower. Colorful butterfly orchids appear to hover in mid-air as they sprout from trees. Leafless ghost orchids grow from speckled snake-like roots, into big, waxy blooms.

In the early years of the Everglades, some wild orchids weighed as much as 50 pounds each! Today, you can find an orchid called the cyrtopodium punctatum that grows to be two to three feet wide.

In other parts of the Everglades, wild pickerel weeds with buds of blue flowers attract grazing deer. Hanging gardens of air plants cling to the forest trees. These unusual plants live off the dust in the air instead of dirt from the ground. Soft, lavender flowers called bull thistle pepper the grass with color, while graceful water lilies decorate the ponds.

FUN FACT The brown pelican hits the water so hard when it dives for fish, the sound can be heard a quarter of a mile away.

A wild bromeliad grows at the base of a cypress tree.

A favorite of tourists is the passion flower. It grows from a woody vine and its leaves are the only food the Zebra butterfly will eat.

A visitor exploring the Everglades will find hundreds of sweet-smelling flowers. The warm tropical air is rich with the fragrance of their perfume.

INSECT LIFE AND SNAILS

Visitors to the Everglades need to bring along good insect repellent. Mosquitoes and horseflies thrive in the warm, wet, tropical glades, especially in the heat of the summer. The golden orb spider is one inhabitant of the Everglades. The web of this very large yellow-and-brown spider is made of tough, silky yellow strands. The strands are as tough as piano wire.

Everglades National Park, which was declared a bird sanctuary, is home to the snowy egret.

They are so sticky that the spider has to be careful not to get caught in its own web! The female golden orb spider will eat her mate, and young spiders eat each other. Only the strongest of the young survive.

In the water, snails are an important link in the Everglades food chain. Apple snails, for example, are the only food for the snail kite. It is common to see a kite using one foot to grab a snail from the water. Nearby farms, canals, and cities, however, are upsetting the wet and dry cycle of the swamp and destroying the snail population. If the glades are too dry, the snails can't live. If the glades are too wet, the snails are eaten by fish, or else they rot in the water.

FUN FACT The silk strands of the golden orb spider are stronger than those of the silkworm. People have made fishnets out of them by twisting the strands together. They also weave a beautiful cloth out of the web.

Hammocks serve as home base for the liguus snail. These tree snails have shells of more than 50 different colors. They eat the *lichen* that grows on tree bark. When people began destroying the hardwood hammocks for their wood, the snails were in danger of disappearing. Fortunately, park rangers saved the snails by moving them deeper into the park.

RIVERS OF FISH

The Everglades has more kinds of fish than any other swamp region in the world. Many of the fish have ancestors who lived in the swamp hundreds of years ago. Now that much of the swampland has been drained, some fish are more difficult to find. The bottlenosed dolphin is a rare sight. The dolphin is a water-dwelling mammal. It frolics in the coastal waters and tidal rivers. As it swims, it leaps and plays with boats that pass by.

Not very long ago fishermen were taking too many fish out of the lakes and rivers of the Everglades. Today, fishing is closely monitored.

Some of the best fishing spots are down by the mangrove forests. There the edge of the swamp meets the Florida Bay. People catch silver king tarpon, snook, sea trout, red fish, mackerel, snapper, and tripletail. Other more dangerous fish are the sharks and barracudas. Both have razor-sharp teeth.

In the ponds and wet lands, fish are an important source of food for other animals. Alligators, crocodiles, birds, bears, raccoons, and snakes all depend on fish to stay alive. During the rainy season, the waters are rich with fish. If you were to journey underwater, you might see a 30-pound channel catfish swim slowly by. Or you might discover the albino catfish, which was first brought into the Everglades by humans. The albino catfish can swim in the water and walk on dry land!

Tiny glass shrimp, crayfish, garfish, needlefish, and wriggly mud eels also share the underwater world of the swamp. During the dry season, many fish disappear into watery solution holes and tunnels in the limestone base. There they live less active lives while waiting for the water level to rise. When the rains come, water pours into dry river beds and shallow ponds. Before too long, water is restored to the Everglades, and rivers of fish flow freely once again.

FUN FACT The female mosquito fish is slightly longer than the male. An adult eats its own weight's worth of mosquito larvae everyday.

The alligator (shown above) has a rounder snout than the crocodile.

REPTILES OF THE EVERGLADES

Reptiles have made their home in the Everglades for centuries. In fact, the slow, lumbering land tortoise has ancestors that lived in the swamp 40 million years ago.

Of all the reptiles in the Everglades, the snakes are the easiest to find. There are 27 kinds of snakes, but only four kinds are poisonous. The yellow-brown diamond-back rattlesnake lives in an underground den. Measuring more than ten feet long, it is the largest poisonous snake in North America. When hungry, it searches for rats, deer mice, or marsh rabbits.

The deadly cotton mouth snake (also called the water moccasin) glides through the waters along the canals. It can loop itself over tree branches to take a quick nap, or coil itself inside a hollow tree stump. The pigmy rattlesnake and the gleaming banded coral snake are also poisonous snakes to stay away from.

A large gentle snake of the Everglades is the shiny blue indigo snake. It might grow to be ten feet long. The six-foot Florida king snake lives on the ground. This speckled snake eats other snakes, even poisonous ones.

Reptiles are cold-blooded, which means they need warmth to stay active. When they are active they hunt, mate, and lay eggs. Turtles like to laze in the mud and soak up sun. One small reptile that changes its color when it is warm or cold is the anole, or false chameleon. This slender green creature turns brown or grey if it is cold or afraid.

Perhaps the largest lizard-like reptiles in the Everglades are the crocodiles and the alligators. They have survived since the days of the dinosaurs.

The crocodiles of the Everglades are the last of their kind in the United States. They live in the salt waters of the mainland bays, along Florida's south shore. There are only a few crocodiles left, and they are protected by law. The sight of one is very rare.

Crocodiles are shy creatures. They lay their eggs in nests along the seashore. Park rangers keep people out of the nesting area to stop *poachers* and people who steal or destroy the eggs.

The alligator has a rounder snout than its distant cousin. Unlike the crocodile, the alligator needs freshwater. For a better look at this crafty reptile, let's take a closer look at the 'gator hole.

THE ALLIGATOR

Like the crocodile, the alligator has faced danger from people in the past. It was slaughtered for its tough skin, so people could have alligator shoes and purses. More than 80% of Florida's alligators were killed. Today, with laws protecting them from human hunters, the number of alligators is increasing again.

The alligator got its name from early Spanish explorers. They called it "el largarto," which means "the lizard." Like the lizard, the alligator spends

FUN FACT The scissor-tailed fly catcher is a bird that got its name because it has a six- to eight-inch-long tail that is shaped like scissors.

a lot of time lying in the sun soaking up the warmth. When it goes into the water, transparent eyelids close over its big yellow eyes. It also has built-in valves in its nose and ears to keep water out.

Although the alligator eats mostly fish, it has been known to go after prey as large as the white-tailed deer. You might wonder how it can catch such quick-footed prey, but with short bursts of energy the alligator can move up to 35 miles per hour!

The mother alligator lays her eggs in late May or early June. She makes a nest in the sawgrass and lays between 30 to 40 eggs. She covers them with sticks and leaves, making a three-foot-high mound. Then she waits near the nest for nine weeks. If anything threatens the safety of her nursery, she roars and bellows until the enemy has been scared away.

When the young are ready to hatch, they start pecking at the shells and making grunting noises. The mother hears them and digs them out of the nest. Even though the alligator can snap its jaws shut with 1,000 pounds of pressure, she gently breaks the shells open with her mouth. Most of the 30 to 40 eggs hatch, but only a handful of those make it to adulthood. A baby alligator is only about one foot long. The mother doesn't feed them, but she will stay and protect them for as long as two years. There in the protected den of its mother, the baby alligator hunts. It eats fish, birds, or any small animal that gets too close to its hungry little jaws.

IN THE ALLIGATOR DEN

Deep in the heart of the swamp, the alligator rules its den. Many of the small ponds and watery hollows in the Everglades are made by the busy alligator. With jaws that can crush metal and a tail that can break a person's legs, its strength is mighty indeed.

The 'gator uses its powerful jaws and tail to slash sawgrass and drag roots, plants, and muck out of the pond. This helps it clear a comfortable home for itself. Under the pond, the den tunnel can be anywhere from 10 to 30 feet long. The mud and plants the alligator removes from its pond help to form a bank. New trees and plants sprout in this bank. After many years they grow into a tangled hedge that birds and other wildlife enjoy.

This process of creating more pond space is very important to the balance

Alligators clear out ponds to make comfortable homes for themselves.

of waterlife in the Everglades, especially during the dry season. The alligator's new pond space attracts more fish, insects, and snails. These creatures are an important source of food for other wildlife. This new food supply is also handy for the alligator's own daily meals.

RAINFALL AND THE DRY SEASON

The wet and dry seasons of the Everglades have a strong effect on the lives of all wildlife. It is important to understand how these cycles affect what happens in the Everglades.

The wet season in the Everglades lasts from May through November. During this time of warmth and endless rains, new life is created. Fish hatch, song birds nest, wild animals mate and raise their young. The hammocks and marshlands are thick with growing plants and new flowers.

The extra rain water of this season is trapped in solution holes and layers of *limestone*. There it is "stored" for use during the dry season.

As the dry season draws near, the water level drops and water drains through holes in the honeycombed limestone bottom. Life seems to dry up with the sun. Many animals are forced to travel to other parts of the Everglades. Over the years, the swamp has adjusted to change. A squishy, grey scum that floats on top of the water holds moisture like a sponge. During the dry season, the scum keeps fish eggs and tiny water creatures alive.

Some creatures like the crayfish burrow into the mud. The salamander makes a chamber out of drying mud, lines it with wet slime and waits for the water to return.

People are affected by the dry season, too. The huge city of Miami is only 35 miles away. When the Everglades dry up, Miami loses a lot of its drinking water. The freshwater begins to disappear, and salt water from the nearby sea starts to seep into the drinking wells.

Problems may also develop during the wet season. Too much rain can hurt the swamp. Lakes and canals flood the plains and drown plants and animals.

Tropical storms, like *hurricanes,* bring great disaster. Powerful winds tear

FUN FACT   The fruit of the soap berry vine can be crushed and mixed with water
to make a good lather for washing. It is every bit as good as store soap!

26

trees up by the roots and blow buildings over. Ocean waters from Florida Bay overflow and bring walls of swirling water into the park. In 1928 a hurricane caused 2,000 deaths and left only six buildings standing in a town called Belle Glade. A lot of animals died, too. In the summer of 1966 more than 5,000 deer were lost as flood waters covered the area.

Throughout the year, raging fires are started by lightning. During the wet season, the fires burn away old trees and dried sawgrass, and their ashes enrich the earth. The soil is protected from damaging heat by the surface water that covers the glades. Fires that spread during the dry season, however, cause much damage to the soil. They burn for days and blacken the land.

Somehow, the Everglades always return to normal, and new life beings its cycle again.

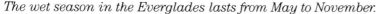

The wet season in the Everglades lasts from May to November.

Many plants store water and many animals burrow into the mud so they can survive the dry season.

SWAMP OF THE SEA

In mangrove country at the edge of the Everglades, the land is at war with the sea. Every day, the battle among water, wind, and land changes the shape of the shore. At high tide, water and wind *erode* the land. The waves leave swirling mounds of sea shells in piles on the beach. Seagulls search for food. Sand bars break the waves, and shell bars produce oysters that are good to eat.

The wind-torn beach of Cape Sable, on the southwest tip of Florida, is left natural by the park rangers. There are no programs to change or improve this area. It is for nature to shape in its own way. Here at the cape, hurricanes have left a history of destruction. Winds reaching 200 miles per hour rip the bark off trees and crush stands of plants. Waves 20 feet high send water

FUN FACT   The wild pine air plant is related to the pineapple. In its leaves it holds water like a cup for animals to drink from.

crashing inland, sometimes as far as ten miles into the shore. The water sucks away the soil and knocks down giant trees. When the storm is over, the cape begins to renew itself. New trees sprout. Animals and birds return to make homes. The Everglade shores reshape themselves.

The creatures who live by the sea make good homes out of the swampy sea habitat. The loggerhead turtle digs a nest in the sand with its powerful flippers. There it lays up to 100 eggs. When the baby turtles hatch, they are only two inches long. They immediately head for the sea and begin their growth into adults. If they aren't eaten first, they may grow to be 500 pounds.

Smaller creatures also make their homes by the sandy shore. Quick, peppy fiddler crabs dig in the sand for food. They help trees grow by opening up the soil with tiny air holes. This helps tree roots breathe.

The horseshoe crab has an interesting way of getting around. When it wants to move, it hurries across the sand on its mouth!

Out in the bay, the rare manatee or sea cow feeds on grass-like sea plants

The Everglades end in Florida Bay, which is at the southern tip of Florida.

that grow close to shore. It can also be seen in river inlets where the salt water mixes with freshwater. An adult manatee can weigh as much as 2,000 pounds. Most of its time is spent in the deep water. It paddles with two front flippers and moves forward with a wide pump-like tail. The manatee comes to the surface every now and then to breathe air. Fishermen have been surprised by a manatee that comes to the surface to breathe. They don't expect to look into a friendly face with whiskers and cow-like eyes coming up for air!

The plants that grow on sandy ridges by the sea shore are very much like desert plants. The cabbage palm is one tree that grows by the beaches. This plant is a favorite food of the black bear. Other plants, like the yucca plant and a variety of cacti, also sprinkle the beach.

Visitors can explore the waterways of this area by boat. Inland, the waterway trails are marked for canoes or small power boats. Many of the trails lead around the Ten Thousand Island area of the park. This wild sea-swamp is an exciting place where visitors can see nature at work.

SWAMP MYSTERIES

The Everglades is a place of mystery and legend. Although the Everglades has changed over the years, much of the mystery still awaits the curious adventurer. Imagine entering the swamp. Everywhere, there are crashing sounds of animals moving through tangled webs of vines and thick brush. Going farther in, there are surprising discoveries.

You might come upon a tree wrapped in the grip of a killing vine called the strangler fig. The strangler fig begins as just a single vine. First a seed, usually dropped by a bird, sprouts on the *host* tree. It then grows downward and slowly winds itself around the trunk and branches until it chokes the tree to death.

Other strange sights spark the imagination. Four-foot-tall air plants seem to grow in mid-air. Fish and pond creatures that disappear in the dry season seem to magically reappear with a rain.

With all these mysteries, it is easy to see how legends started with early explorers. It is believed that the Everglades legend of mermaids began with the manatee. Although the manatee lives in the water, it is a *mammal* and

The strangler fig is only one of the mysteries of the Everglades.

A wide variety of plants and animals live in the hot and swampy areas of the Everglades.

Manatees are large mammals that live in the waters of Florida Bay.

needs to breathe air. Newborn manatees have to be brought to the surface every few minutes to breathe. The mother holds her pup up with both flippers. She looks like a human mother holding her baby. Sailors, tired and lonesome for home, saw this human-like activity and believed the manatee was half human and half fish. Thus the legend of the mermaid began.

Another mystery is the behavior of the gopher tortoise. This friendly tortoise offers a strange kind of friendship to other creatures in its den. The tortoise digs a deep hole in dry, sandy areas. Other creatures, who are enemies above ground, call a truce underground. Some of the tortoise's guests in the den are spiders and flies, scorpions and lizards, snakes and rats, and raccoons. No one knows why these enemies share living quarters.

The presence of 300-pound wild hogs in the swamp is a puzzle until one learns of their past. These hogs with their wicked, sharp tusks were once tame. Early Spanish explorers raised tame hogs for food. When they came to Florida in search of gold, they brought some along. Some hogs escaped into the forests and became wild. There they learned to survive on their own.

SOUNDS OF THE NIGHT

When the hot summer sun finally sets and the moon rises, cool night air stirs the Everglades. Fog mists the land, and hordes of fireflies light the darkness. Tiny green tree frogs cling to the trees. The moonflower unfolds from a mass of tangled vines, blossoming under the soft moonlight.

On the south border of the park the wind rustles the mangrove trees, causing heavy string bean-shaped pods to splash into the water below. Raccoons ripple the waters as they pry coon oysters from the mangrove prop roots.

Far up on the northern border, the cry of the limpkin bird lingers. A black bear scratches its back on the tree bark. An alligator bellows, thrashing in its pond. A chorus of croaking leopard frogs add their voices to the noise of the bullfrog.

In the night sky bats swoop and catch their supper from thick clouds of mosquitoes. Night herons splash as they hunt in the dark ponds for fish. Wild cats prowl in search of food. The heavy smell of swamp gases fills the air.

A night in the Everglades is also an interesting experience during the winter season when there aren't as many bugs. The Everglades rangers offer campfire programs and night prowls into the park. You might see an opossum hanging upside down by its tail from a tree. A fox or a raccoon looking for leftovers may visit a group of night campers. It's wise to be careful and carry a flashlight at night to help enjoy the park in the dark.

THE PEOPLE WHO LIVE IN THE EVERGLADES

In 1513 when the first Spanish explorers came to Florida, Calusa Native Americans controlled the Everglades. They were a fierce tribe and skilled in survival. They had to be, since life in the unexplored swamp was wild and harsh.

Later in history, the Seminole tribe made their home in the Everglades. The word "Seminole" in Native American language means "people that chose to be free." This has special meaning for the Seminoles, since they were the only Native Americans that the United States government never completely defeated.

To protect themselves, the Seminoles disappeared into the swamp to live. They hunted and fished for food to stay alive. The sharp sawgrass and other dangers helped prevent attacks from invading soldiers trying to capture the Seminoles. The government finally gave up, and the Native Americans were free to live in the Everglades.

Relatives of these proud people still live on reservations in the Everglades. Today six separate tribes live close to each other. They are descendants of the Creek and Seminole nations called the Miccosukees (pronounced Mik-oh-soo-keez).

Some of the Miccosukee make a living as cattle ranchers. Some farm while others earn a living as merchants. Some act as guides for canoe trips that lead deep into the Everglades.

Some of the Miccosukees live in traditional thatched roof huts. These huts have open sides and are called *chickees*. Even now they follow many of their ancient tribal customs, and a few Miccosukee men wrestle with alligators for sport!

The Miccosukees are a private people. They often wear colorful tribal

FUN FACT A little known burial ground for the Seminole tribe is found inside lonely hammocks. There they laid their dead to rest in the center of the tree island.

robes. The women are skilled in making hand-crafted wall hangings and colorful bead designs.

The Miccosukee have a great respect for the land. They take good care of their homeland. As one of their legends of the Everglades proclaims, "She (the land) gives us all we need to live. She tells us to take only what is necessary and no more."

TAKING CARE IN THE SWAMP

Today, the Everglades is a national park where people come to explore a tropical wilderness. In the past, hunters and poachers almost killed off many of the beautiful wild creatures. Much of the wilderness was being destroyed. The people of Florida wanted to protect their unique and rare wilderness. In 1947 part of the Everglades was made into a national park.

The Florida panther is one of the beautiful, but endangered, animals of the Everglades.

As a result, there are now many rules to follow in the park. In fact, many parts of the park are closed to visitors. This gives the animals a chance to mate and live without intrusion.

The park protects the wilderness but it also provides opportunities for wilderness fishing, boating, hiking, canoeing, and nature study. Park rangers are always on hand to guide visitors and help solve problems. They also make sure people follow the rules of the park so the natural resources are preserved.

When you go hiking or camping, you must bring out everything that you take in, including pop cans, food wrappers, and other garbage. The same rules apply for the bike trails and the hiking trails.

At Cape Sable, shell collecting is banned and swimming is discouraged. The waters are murky and are home to five kinds of sharks and the southern sting ray. The tide can also be dangerously strong. Those are some good reasons to stay on land or in a canoe!

If visitors remember the rules for safety and wildlife preservation, the park is a great place to enjoy the wilderness.

There are several ways to tour the swamp. You can bicycle through the park or hike along the trails, which are raised, wooden, boardwalks that follow different routes. The Mahogany Hammock trail goes by some of the biggest mahogany trees in the country. The Gumbo Limbo Trail passes through a green jungle of tropical trees and air plants. The Anhinga Trail leads to alligators and wading birds. The Mangrove Trail leads through the mangrove jungles.

For water lovers the Wilderness Waterway is a marked trail that's 99 miles long. It takes visitors past the Ten Thousand Islands and along the mangrove coast.

If you want to get really wet, you can choose to go on a *swamp tromp.* A swamp tromp involves wading through the shallow waters of the swamp in old pants and tennis shoes. Don't forget to take insect repellent and a cap to prevent sunburn! During a swamp tromp visitors can experience the waterlife first hand and take plenty of close-up pictures. A pair of binoculars are helpful for spotting birds and animals.

Visitors can explore the Everglades by walking on raised, wooden boardwalks.

A "Save the Everglades" program was started to protect the environment so birds like the blue heron can live peacefully.

THE FUTURE OF THE EVERGLADES

The Everglades is fighting a continuing battle for survival. People have played an important role in changing the wilderness from a wild frontier into an endangered national wildlife park. Once the Everglades covered over

seven million acres of tropical wilderness, but today only about half of the wilderness remains. Much of the land has been cleared and drained for farms and towns. *Leevees* and huge *reservoirs* keep the water from flowing freely into the swamp. Natural water cycles have been changed forever by the construction of canals and floodgates.

Lake Okeechobee, the main source of water, now has flood control that sends extra water into the ocean. Unfortunately, this reduces the water covering the Everglades. This affects the birds, fish, and animal population

Exploring the Everglades is always a fascinating adventure.

of the park.

Miami is growing so fast that it is using up water the Everglades needs. This has started a drying trend and threatens the wildlife that depends on the high water levels of the wet season.

Many endangered animals can't have a successful mating season because the changes are too upsetting. Concerned people have started a "Save the Everglades" program to try to get water flowing back into the park.

The richness and variety of wildlife in the Everglades are like nowhere else on earth. People must learn to care for the park and help the wilderness survive. Without care, the Everglades may disappear forever.

There is much to explore and many mysteries still to uncover. You are always on the brink of discovery in this tropical land of the Everglades.

FOR MORE PARK INFORMATION

For more information about Everglades National Park, write to:

Superintendent
Everglades National Park
Box 279
Homestead, FL 33030

PARK MAP

Ten Thousand Islands

Highway 41

Highway 27

Mahogany Hammock

Gumbo Limbo Trail

Anhinga Trail

Park Headquarters & Visitor Center

Gulf of Mexico

Cape Sable

Mangrove Trail

Visitor Center

Atlantic Ocean

Florida Bay

Everglades National Park

GLOSSARY/INDEX

CANAL *7, 41*—A pathway for water to flow through.

CHICKEE *36*—An open-sided hut made by the Miccosukees.

CYPRESS KNEES *10*—Pointed roots of the cypress trees that poke up out of the water.

ENDANGERED *40, 44*—Plants and animals in danger of disappearing forever.

ERODE *28*—To wear away the land.

HABITAT *29*—A place where things grow or live naturally.

HAMMOCK *7, 11, 18, 21, 26*—A raised piece of land with hardwood trees growing on it.

HOST *30*—Any plant or animal on which another lives for protection or food.

HURRICANE *8, 14, 26*—A violent tropical storm with dangerous winds.

LEGEND *30*—A story that people have told for generations.

LEVEE *41*—A bank built to keep high water from flooding the land.

LICHEN *21*—Small fungus plants.

LIMESTONE *26*—A soft stone made from the skeletons of sea creatures who died millions of years ago.

MAMMAL *21, 30*—A warm-blooded animal that feeds its offspring milk.

MICCOSUKEE *36*—The name of a Native American tribe native to the Everglades.

PARK RANGER *23, 28, 38*—People who take care of the park.

POACHERS *23*—People who hunt or catch game against the law.

PREY *5, 14, 25*—An animal hunted for food by other animals.

PROP ROOTS *11*—The arched roots of the mangrove tree.

REPTILE *22, 23*—Cold-blooded creatures that have lungs.

RESERVOIR *41*—A place where water is collected and stored.

RESIN *14*—Sticky sap from a cut in a tree.

SEMINOLE *7, 36*—A Native American tribe that lives in the Everglades.

SLOUGHS *7*—A hole in the ground full of deep, soft mud.

SWAMP TROMP *38*—A hike visitors can take to study nature by wading through the water with a park ranger.